Workshop on NLP and Pseudonymisation 2019

NEALT Proceedings Series Volume 41

Turku, Finland
30 September 2019

Editors:

Lars Ahrenberg
Beáta Megyesi

ISBN: 978-1-5108-9445-7

Printed from e-media with permission by:

Curran Associates, Inc.
57 Morehouse Lane
Red Hook, NY 12571

Some format issues inherent in the e-media version may also appear in this print version.

Printed by Curran Associates, Inc. (2019)

For permission requests, please contact the Association for Computational Linguistics at the address below.

Association for Computational Linguistics
209 N. Eighth Street
Stroudsburg, Pennsylvania 18360

Phone: 1-570-476-8006
Fax: 1-570-476-0860

acl@aclweb.org

Additional copies of this publication are available from:

Curran Associates, Inc.
57 Morehouse Lane
Red Hook, NY 12571 USA
Phone: 845-758-0400
Fax: 845-758-2633
Email: curran@proceedings.com
Web: www.proceedings.com

The Northern European Association for Language Technology

Workshop on NLP and Pseudonymisation Proceedings

image: Turku Castle, Turku, Finland by Joakim Honkasalo @jhonkasalo.
url: https://unsplash.com/photos/OitUG45b51Y

Editors: Lars Ahrenberg and Beáta Megyesi

NODALIDA 2019
September 30, 2019
Turku, Finland

Proceedings of the Workshop on NLP and Pseudonymisation

Editors: Lars Ahrenberg and Beáta Megyesi

September 30, 2019
Turku, Finland

Published by
Linköping University Electronic Press, Sweden
Linköping Electronic Conference Proceedings, No. 166
Series: NEALT Proceedings Series, No. 41

ISSN: 1650-3686
eISSN: 1650-3740

Preface

The goal of making research data freely available often comes into conflict with the rights of individuals. These rights are mainly of two kinds: intellectual property rights and rights to personal data protection. In Europe, the rights to personal data protection have been codified in the recently adopted General Data Protection Regulation, GDPR. While research, as a public interest, can process personal data, the GDPR requires appropriate safeguards to be in place. Consent from authors or subjects cannot always be obtained, or be general enough, and in this case pseudonymisation may be applied, with the intended effect that real individuals no longer can be identified from the language data.

Long before the GDPR, personal data protection has been a concern for creators of language corpora, and there exists a body of literature discussing legal and ethical aspects of corpus publishing. When the data is to be changed or masked in some way, the terms used have been anonymisation or de-identification. With textual data, originals are usually kept, however, which means that anyone with access to the originals and their metadata can make the connection with the transformed text and thus with individuals as authors or participants. For this reason we have used the GDPR term and called this workshop 'NLP for Pseudonymisation'.

NLP is affected in two ways by the conflict. First, it uses language data of all kinds to develop systems, and these data may contain sensitive personal data. Second, it may contribute to making the pseudonymisation process more efficient, or even, more safe. We invited submissions on both of these aspects to the workshop.

NLP has been applied to the problem of deidentification of medical texts for quite a long time. Two of the three papers included in these proceedings deal with medical data. Moreover, in medicine, taxonomies of sensitive data categories are well established and annotated data already in existence. Many other fields, however, not least in the Humanities and Social Sciences, are increasingly aiming to share human-generated data and will need to develop tools and processes for this purpose. We hope that future workshops on the theme of NLP and Pseudonymisation will have a wider spread of contributions.

We would like to express our gratitude to the members of the program committee for their valuable advise and review of papers: Hercules Dalianis, Koenraad de Smedt, Cyril Grouin, Dimitrios Kokkinakis, Krister Lindén, Aurélie Névéol, Sumithra Velupillai, Sussi Olsen, Elena Volodina, and Mats Wirén. We gratefully acknowledge financial support for the workshop from Swe-Clarin, the Swedish node of the European CLARIN infrastructure, with long-term support from the Swedish Research Council.

Linköping and Uppsala, August 26, 2019

Lars Ahrenberg and Beáta Megyesi
Program co-chairs

Program Committee

Lars Ahrenberg (program co-chair), Linköping University, Sweden
Beáta Megyesi (program co-chair), Uppsala University, Sweden
Hercules Dalianis, Stockholm University, Sweden
Koenraad de Smedt, University of Bergen, Norway
Cyril Grouin, LIMSI, CNRS, Université Paris-Saclay, France
Dimitrios Kokkinakis, University of Gothenburg, Sweden
Krister Lindén, University of Helsinki, Finland
Aurélie Névéol, LIMSI, CNRS, Université Paris-Saclay, France
Sumithra Velupillai, King's College, London, UK
Sussi Olsen, CST, University of Copenhagen, Denmark
Elena Volodina, University of Gothenburg, Sweden
Mats Wirén, Stockholm University, Sweden

Invited talk

Martin Krallinger

Head of the Text Mining unit, Barcelona Supercomputing Center (BSC), Spain

Abstract

There is an increasing interest in exploiting the content of unstructured clinical narratives by means of language technologies and text mining. To be able to share, re-distribute and make clinical narratives accessible for text mining and NLP research purposes it is key to fulfill legal conditions and address restrictions related data protection and patient privacy legislations. Thus clinical records with protected health information (PHI) cannot be directly shared "as is", due to privacy constraints, making it particularly cumbersome to carry out NLP research in the medical domain. A necessary precondition for accessing clinical records outside of hospitals is their de-identification, i.e., the exhaustive removal (or replacement) of all mentioned PHI phrases.

Providing a proper evaluation scenario of automatic anonymization tools, with well-defined sensitive data types is crucial for approval of data redistribution consents signed by ethical committees of healthcare institutions. Moreover, it is important to highlight that the construction of manually de-identified medical records is currently the main rate and cost-limiting step for secondary use applications.

This talk will summarise the settings, data and results of the first community challenge task specifically devoted to the anonymization of medical documents in Spanish, called the MEDDOCAN (Medical Document Anonymization) task, as part of the upcoming IberLEF evaluation initiative. This track relied on a synthetic corpus of clinical case documents called the MEDDOCAN corpus. In order to carry out the manual annotation of this corpus we have constructed the first public annotation guidelines for PHI in Spanish carefully examining the specifications derived from the EU General Data Protection Regulation (GDPR). From the 51 registered teams, covering participants both from academia and companies, a total of 18 teams have submitted runs for this track. The top scoring runs represent very competitive approaches than can significantly reduce time and costs associated to the access of textual data containing privacy-related sensitive information. This talk will conclude with a summary of the methodologies used by participating teams to automatically identify sensitive information, together with lessons learned and future steps.

Bio

Martin Krallinger is currently the head of the Text Mining unit at the Barcelona Supercomputing Center (BSC), and former head of the Biological Text Mining unit of the Spanish National Cancer research Centre (CNIO). He is an expert in the field of biomedical and clinical text mining and language technologies and has been working in this and related research topics since more than ten years, which resulted in over 70 publications and several domain specific text mining applications for drug-safety, molecular systems biology and oncology, etc. He was involved in the implementation and evaluation of biomedical named entity recognition components, information extraction systems and semantic indexing of large datasets of heterogeneous document types (research literature, patents, legacy reports, European public assessment reports). His research interests, besides clinical NLP include text-mining assisted biocuration, interoperability standards and formats for biomedical text annotations (BioC) as well as development of efficient text annotation infrastructures. He also promoted the development of the first biomedical text annotation meta-server (Biocreative metaserver - BCMS) and the follow up BeCalm/TIPS metaserver. He is one of the main organizers of BioCreative community assessment challenges for the evaluation of biomedical NLP systems and has been involved in the organization of text mining shared tasks in various international community challenge efforts including IberEval, IberLEF, and CLEF.

Contents

Preface v
Invited talk vii

Papers

AnonyMate: A Toolkit for Anonymizing Unstructured Chat Data
Allison Adams, Eric Aili, Daniel Aioanei, Rebecca Jonsson, Lina Mickelsson, Dagmar Mikmekova, Fred Roberts, Javier Fernandez Valencia, Roger Wechsler 1

Augmenting a De-identification System for Swedish Clinical Text Using Open Resources and Deep learning
Hanna Berg and Hercules Dalianis.. 8

Pseudonymisation of Swedish Electronic Patient Records Using a Rule-Based Approach
Hercules Dalianis 16

AnonyMate: A Toolkit for Anonymizing Unstructured Chat Data

Allison Adams, Eric Aili, Daniel Aioanei, Rebecca Jonsson, Lina Mickelsson, Dagmar Mikmekova, Fred Roberts, Javier Fernandez Valencia, Roger Wechsler
Artificial Solutions
Stureplan 15, Stockholm 111 45
r&d@artificial-solutions.com

Abstract

Most existing research on the automatic anonymization of text data has been limited to the de-identification of medical records. This is beginning to change following the passage of GDPR privacy laws, which have made the task of automatic text anonymization more relevant than ever. We present our privacy protection toolkit, AnonyMate, which is built to anonymize both personal identifying information (PII) as well as corporate identifying information (CII) in human-computer dialogue text data.

1 Introduction

Many NLP systems require vast amounts of text data to develop. This poses a considerable challenge to companies who want to prioritize the data integrity and privacy of their clients while building state of the art tools. The General Data Protection Regulation (GDPR) [1] sets restrictions on the usage and storage of personal identifying information (PII), which is often present in human-computer dialog data. As such, steps to remove sensitive information through anonymization are essential if the data are to be collected and stored for research and development purposes. To address this need, we developed our anonymization tool, AnonyMate, with two main objectives in mind:

- To ensure that historical data stored for R&D purposes do not contain any PII data.
- To enable our platform to produce anonymized data.

In light of these objectives, our goal was to build a tool that can identify and classify types of PII data and apply different anonymization and pseudonymization strategies on the detected PII types. We further sought to detect and annotate named entities beyond the scope of anonymization purposes.

The development of this system encompassed a diverse range of tasks including: establishing a tag set of PII and named entity types with guidelines for annotation, the creation of an annotation tool, a large-scale annotation effort in multiple languages, and the testing and implementation of Named Entity Recognition (NER) and language identification systems. The resulting anonymization pipeline comprises five modules: a pre-processing step, a language detector, an NER component, coreference resolution and, finally, an anonymization step, in which identified entities are removed or replaced. In this paper we present an overview of this project and our anonymization pipeline architecture.

2 Tag set and annotation

2.1 Tag set

In the first phase of this project, we established a set of entity types we wanted our system to be able to identify. As our data, sampled from historical chat logs, belong to a diverse set of domains, we identified 24 named entity types we expected to be present in our data. We classified them into three categories:

i. *Personal Identifying Information* (PII), or named entities that could link the data to a specific individual.

ii. *Corporate Identifying Information* (CII), or named entities that could link the data to a specific organization or client.

iii. *Other*, which contain entities we do not expect to anonymize, but nonetheless want to identify in our data.

[1]https://eur-lex.europa.eu/eli/reg/2016/679/oj

Proceedings of the Workshop on NLP and Pseudonymisation, pages 1–7,
Turku, Finland, 30 September 2019. © 2019 Linköping University Electronic Press

PII	CII	Other
Person	Organization	Nationality
Address	Product	Geographical
Zip Code	Facility	Event
Location	URL	Work of Art
Email		Language
UID		Unit
IP Address		Misc
(Date)		Med/Chem
		Sports Team
		Known Group
		Known Figure
		Fictional Figure
		Date

Table 1: Categorization of entity types in our tag set

Table 1 lists these entity types and their respective groupings. The first group, PII, comprises entities relating to an identifiable person. This category includes person names, addresses (including e-mail and IP addresses), zip codes, locations, unique identifiers (UID), which includes entities such as phone numbers or social security numbers, and in some cases birth dates. We further aimed to protect not only the privacy of individuals present in our data, but that of our corporate clients as well. The list of entity types pertaining to CII includes organizations, products, facilities and URLs. Finally, we established a list of named entities we expect to occur frequently in our data that fall outside the scope of this anonymization task. This list includes named entities useful to identify within our platform, for example for slot-filling purposes, such as nationalities, languages, units (when in the context of an amount, e.g. *5 kilometers*), medical/chemical entities, known figures, etc. We also reserved a placeholder *Miscellaneous* tag to annotate things that are clearly named entities but that do not fit in any other category, such as *What is the 50th digit of* ***Pi*** or *When did the* ***Titanic*** *sink?*.

2.2 Data selection and pre-annotation

We expected named entities to be somewhat sparsely represented in our data and, as such, to speed up the annotation process, we sought to develop a method of pre-selecting sentences for our training set that had a higher likelihood of containing a named entity. Lingren et al., 2013 have demonstrated dictionary-based annotation methods to save time on NER annotation tasks without introducing bias to the annotation process. Following these findings, we used our in-house lexical resources to develop a rule-based and dictionary-based method for identifying inputs likely to contain an entity. This system further acts as a simplistic NER tagger that pre-annotates the data.

2.3 Annotation guidelines and training

More than 15 annotators contributed to the development of our annotated NER data set, working in 6 languages (English, German, Swedish, Spanish, Italian and French). To coordinate this annotation effort we established a set of guidelines for each language, designed to be as synchronized as possible across all development languages. As a part of these guidelines, we instructed annotators to:

- Tag according to context, selecting the most obvious and probable meaning or tag in cases of ambiguous inputs (e.g. *I paid with my visa_PRODUCT* vs. *Visa_ORGANIZATION is a credit card company.*).
- Follow word boundaries in the case of compounds. This means that in English, for example, we only annotate the named entity part of the compound in *visa_PRODUCT card_X* while for Swedish *visakort_PRODUCT*, the whole compound is annotated.
- Generally, determiners are not to be included in the scope of an entity. Only annotate determiners (or other function words) if they are part of the official name of an entity, e.g. *I read the_PRODUCT times_PRODUCT*.

We further established recommendations for tags such as *Work of Art* or *Known Figure*, which require the annotator to make a subjective judgment. These guidelines include rules of thumb for what or who does or does not constitute a work of art or a known figure, where to draw the distinction between a geographical entity or a location, etc. As we used IOB encoding (Ramshaw and Marcus, 1999), a text chunking format used to denote the scope of entity chunks, to annotate our data set, we also provided instructions to our annotators on determining the start and end of an entity.

	Training Set			Test Set		
	Entities	Tokens	Sentences	Entities	Tokens	Sentences
English	62231	586637	61081	5217	51078	5097
French	33075	382099	28033	5889	60646	4914
German	73052	570527	78261	4083	30768	3949
Italian	42494	404078	39609	5565	50730	4589
Spanish	35583	357045	34684	4495	34451	4437
Swedish	53218	524703	60830	2862	24006	2763

Table 2: Training and test data set size by language

After establishing our tag set and annotation guidelines, we held training sessions with our annotators, who we in turn tasked with annotating a 300 sentence subset of the training data. We then collectively discussed the sentences for which our annotators had produced different annotations, revisiting problematic tags and reviewing the guidelines. As an additional step to improve inter-annotator agreement, we encouraged annotators to work collaboratively to reach joint decisions about difficult or ambiguous tags.

To evaluate inter-annotator agreement, we measured agreement separately for every pair of annotators on the 300 double-annotated sentences of the training set using Cohen's kappa (Cohen, 1960) and report the average score. These results are shown in Table 3.

	Average κ	Annotators
English	.89	9
French	.89	3
German	.84	6
Italian	.89	2
Spanish	.75	4
Swedish	.90	5

Table 3: Average Cohen's kappa for inter-annotator agreement

2.4 Annotation tool

In addition to receiving training in our annotation guidelines, our annotators were also instructed on how to use our web-based tool developed in-house to facilitate the process of annotating written language data. In the annotation tool user interface, the annotator chooses the appropriate label for each word in a sentence from a drop-down menu. The tool also allows the annotator to navigate through examples, giving them the option to skip tricky examples and revisit them later.

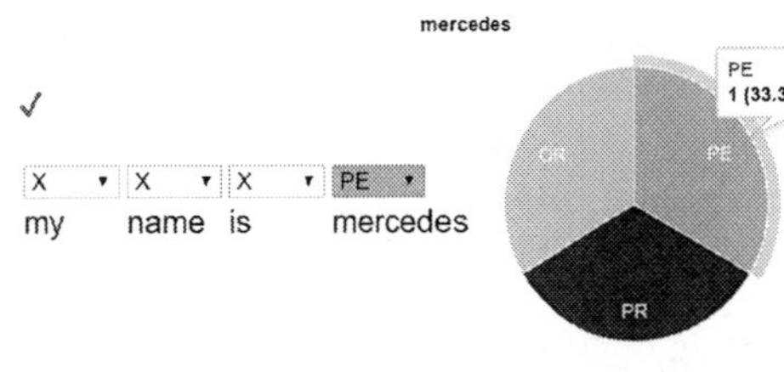

Figure 1: Annotation tool user interface

In order to ensure consistent annotation, the tool displays statistics for how a given word has been annotated previously. For instance, in the hypothetical example shown in Figure 1, the annotator can see that the ambiguous token, *Mercedes*, has been marked as a product, organization, and as a person. A regex search function then allows the user to review previous examples to see the context in which these tags were assigned.

2.5 Data sets composition

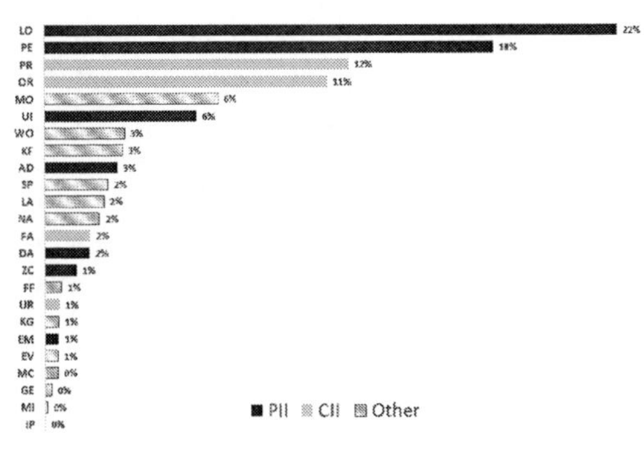

Figure 2: Distribution of named entity tags in the English training set

Table 2 features the training and test set sizes for the six languages we developed. The table lists the number of entities, tokens, and sentences that each data set contains. Our training data sets range in size from 28,033 sentences for French, to 78,261 for German. We did not necessarily expect a correlation between training data set size and NER model performance, as our larger data sets tend to contain a broader range of domains, which we expected to make them more difficult to predict.

Our English training data set contains 61,081 sentences, 585,773 tokens and 62,231 annotated entities. Figure 2 shows the distribution of named entity tag types in the English training data set. We generally observed very similar distribution pattern across all languages we developed. We opted to maintain the natural distribution of entity types in our data set, rather than artificially inflate the training set for underrepresented tag types. As Figure 2 shows, PII and CII tags occur most frequently in the data, with the exception of URLs, IP addresses and E-mail addresses. Given the predictability of these entity forms, however, we did not expect their lack of frequency in the training data to be problematic.

3 Named entity recognition for anonymization

Named entity recognition (NER), the identification of named entities in unstructured text, is a standard component of anonymization and de-identification systems. Most prior research in automatic text anonymization has focused on the de-identification of medical records, and has employed either rule-based (Ruch et al., 2000; Neamatullah et al., 2008) or machine learning (Guo et al., 2006; Yang and Garibaldi, 2015) NER techniques. For the purposes of our system, we opted for the latter and explored two different NER system architectures: one based on conditional random fields (CRFs) and the other using deep-learning techniques based on the model proposed by Lample et al., 2016, which is a BiLSTM with a CRF decoding layer. We developed the CRF model using CRFSuite (Okazaki, 2007). The neural network model was implemented in Tensorflow (Abadi et al., 2015).

In addition to using word, basic prefix and suffix, as well as regex features to help detect e-mail addresses and series of digits, one CRFSuite model makes use of embeddings clusters, which we derived by performing K-means clustering on word embeddings, which we trained on our own in-house data using Word2Vec (Mikolov et al., 2013). In doing so, our aim was to group together words which are distributionally similar in order to imbue our model with some degree of semantic understanding, while maintaining the model size small relative to using the full emebeddings model.

3.1 NER performance

SYSTEM TYPE	F1
Baseline (unamb)	45.0
Baseline (freq)	57.5
CRFSuite	74.1
CRFSuite + embeddings clusters	76.0
BiLSTM + CRF decoding	**79.2**

Table 4: NER system performance for English

Table 4 shows the results of an evaluation of our English NER models on a separate test set. We performed our evaluation following the same methods used in the CoNLL-2003 shared task on named entity recognition (Sang and De Meulder, 2003). The test set contains 5,217 entities, and comprises 51,078 tokens and 5,097 sentences, making it slightly less than 10 percent the size of the training set. We evaluated our models against two baseline metrics; an unambiguous baseline (unamb), in which entities that appear in the training set with only one annotation are assigned that label in the test set, and a frequency-based baseline (freq), in which entities that appear in the training set are assigned the most frequent annotation that the entity was given in the training set. All three models we investigated performed well over these baselines, with the highest performing model being our neural network based system. We further see that the use of embeddings clusters in the CRFSuite model results in a modest improvement in F1 compared to not using the embeddings clusters. We used default parameters when training and testing these models, so it is possible that tuning could lead to further improvements over the baseline.

Figure 3 shows the F1 per named entity tag of the CRFSuite model with word embeddings clusters for English. The highest performing entity types benefit from our regex pattern matching feature, which identifies sequences of digits and special characters. Moreoever, we see F1 scores of 75% and above for all PII entity types, and 70% and above for all CII entity types. Table 5 shows averaged precision, recall and F1 for PII

	PII			CII		
LANGUAGE	P	R	F1	P	R	F1
English	86.4	82.7	84.6	87.0	73.5	79.5
French	89.4	89.4	89.3	85.3	78.0	81.0
German	92.7	89.6	91.1	86.5	65.5	73.5
Italian	88.7	86.0	87.1	87.5	73.0	77.8
Swedish	89.1	83.7	86.1	84.5	71.5	77.0
Spanish	89.1	86.9	87.7	89.3	80.5	84.5

Table 5: Average PII and CII performance: English CRFSuite with embeddings clusters

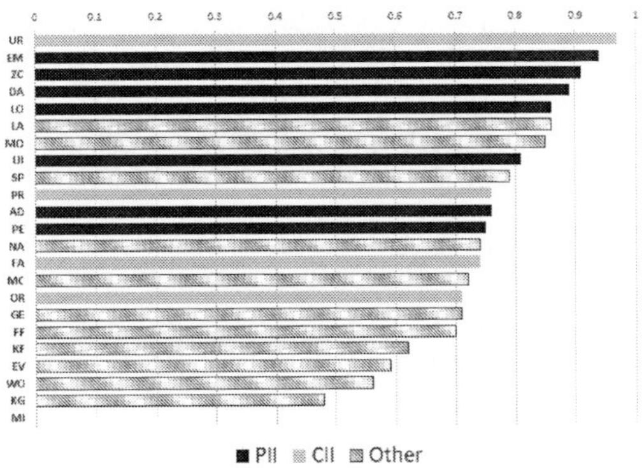

Figure 3: Performance of English CRFSuite with embeddings clusters, by named entity type

and CII for each language. As the table shows, both PII and CII types perform well above the average model F1. Our evaluations are carried out on the chunk level, rather than on token level, and we observe that scores are generally lower for tags likely to contain multi-token entities (e.g. personal names, addresses, facilities, organizations, etc.). A point of further investigation is to perform an error analysis on these entity types, as even partial recognition of an entity chunk is likely to be sufficient for anonymization purposes. We further observe a correlation between entity tag frequency in the data set and performance, suggesting that the performance of some tags could be improved through the addition of training data for these entity types. As IP addresses were generally lacking from our data set, we opted to remove this tag from our NER training set and use regular expressions instead of relying on NER.

Finally, Table 6 shows the performance of the CRFSuite model with embeddings clusters for each language as compared to the two baseline evaluation metrics. As the table shows, the models for all languages performed well over both baselines. We do, however, see that performance gains over the baseline are more modest for the languages for which we have less training data.

LANGUAGE	**CRF**	**Freq.**	**Unamb.**
English	76.0	57.5	45.0
French	84.9	75.3	64.5
German	85.4	70.8	59.1
Italian	83.8	72.9	67.7
Spanish	80.8	68.9	57.7
Swedish	76.5	62.5	52.8

Table 6: NER performance by language: CRFSuite with embeddings clusters

4 Language detector

Given that our anonymization pipelines are language-specific, in order to ensure we anonymize our data effectively, we developed an automatic language identification system to confirm that inputs are being sent into the correct NER pipeline. Our data are organized according to project, which are typically monolingual, however we expect a certain amount of noise in the data, and want to be sure that we do not fail to anonymize PII based on this factor.

Our language detector is currently capable of predicting 45 languages and was trained using OpenNLP's (Apache Software Foundation, 2014) language detector model (a Naïve Bayes Classifier) on a training set of 182,087 sentences. We sourced the training data from a combination of in-house project data as well as external corpora, namely, the OpenSubtitles (Tiedemann, 2016) and Europarl (Koehn, 2005) corpora. We cleaned our in-house data in the following ways:

- An initial coarse regex-based method to identify English inputs based on frequently occurring words (e.g. *Hello*, *would*, *could*, etc.).

- Analyzing a preliminary model's output on the data set using cross-validation to identify sentences incorrectly classified as false positives.

These adjustments to our training data resulted in a final F1 of 93.01% tested on separate test set of 19,828 sentences.

5 Coreference resolution

The last stage in our pipeline before anonymization handles basic coreference resolution. This system keeps track of multiple occurrences of entities on a user chat session level. For example, if a user refers to the same person name multiple times throughout a chat session, the name is anonymized to *Person 1*. If a user then mentions a second name during the course of a session, that name is then anonymized to *Person 2*. This allows us to maintain the distinction between different individuals while protecting the privacy of those discussed over the course of a full dialogue.

6 Anonymization pipeline

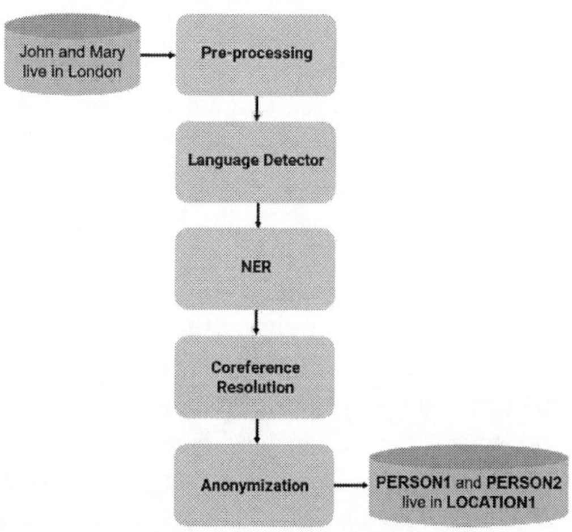

Figure 4: Anonymization pipeline architecture

Figure 4 shows the AnonyMate pipeline architecture. An input is first sent to a pre-processing module which deunicodes, removes non-printable characters, and strips HTML tags before tokenizing the input. The input is then sent to the language detector. Inputs identified as foreign are deleted from our logs rather than being sent to the NER module. Depending on the settings selected, the input can be sent either to be processed by a BiLSTM+CRF NER module or a CRF NER module. Finally, after the input has been analyzed for entities, coreference resolution is applied to the input.

The anonymization strategy applied is configurable by the user, where the user can select which entity types to anonymize. Moreover, the tool allows the option to suppress certain entity types, whereby entities are simply removed from the input (e.g. *I live in London.* $\rightarrow$ *I live in **** .); tag entities, in which entities are replaced with their named entity tag (e.g. *I live in London.* $\rightarrow$ *I live in LOCATION.*); or substitute entities, in which a specific entity is replaced by a predetermined string (e.g. *I live in London.* $\rightarrow$ *I live in ENGLISH_CITY.*)

7 Conclusion

In this paper we have presented an overview of our anonymization toolkit, AnonyMate, and detailed the stages of the project. We have described the creation of a tag set and data set used to train and test a named entity recognition system that can be applied to the tasks of anonymization and slot-filling, as well as given an evaluation of the NER systems we developed. We further reported on the implementation of a language detection system used to filter foreign inputs that our language-specific anonymization pipeline would fail to successfully de-identify. Finally, we provided a description of the anonymization pipeline architecture, and discussed the various strategies employed to remove personal and corporate identifying information from our data. AnonyMate has given us the ability to both remove PII and CII data from our historical data, so that they can be stored for future use in research and development, as well as enabled our platform to generate anonymized data.

Acknowledgments

We would like to thank our annotators for their hard work and dedication in creating our data sets, as well as the three reviewers for their valuable comments.

References

Martín Abadi, Ashish Agarwal, Paul Barham, Eugene Brevdo, Zhifeng Chen, Craig Citro, Greg S. Corrado, Andy Davis, Jeffrey Dean, Matthieu Devin, Sanjay Ghemawat, Ian Goodfellow, Andrew Harp,

Geoffrey Irving, Michael Isard, Yangqing Jia, Rafal Jozefowicz, Lukasz Kaiser, Manjunath Kudlur, Josh Levenberg, Dan Mané, Rajat Monga, Sherry Moore, Derek Murray, Chris Olah, Mike Schuster, Jonathon Shlens, Benoit Steiner, Ilya Sutskever, Kunal Talwar, Paul Tucker, Vincent Vanhoucke, Vijay Vasudevan, Fernanda Viégas, Oriol Vinyals, Pete Warden, Martin Wattenberg, Martin Wicke, Yuan Yu, and Xiaoqiang Zheng. 2015. http://tensorflow.org/ TensorFlow: Large-scale machine learning on heterogeneous systems. Software available from tensorflow.org.

Apache Software Foundation. 2014. http://opennlp.apache.org/ openNLP Natural Language Processing Library. Http://opennlp.apache.org/.

Jacob Cohen. 1960. A coefficient of agreement for nominal scales. *Educational and psychological measurement*, 20(1):37–46.

Yikun Guo, Robert Gaizauskas, Ian Roberts, George Demetriou, Mark Hepple, et al. 2006. Identifying personal health information using support vector machines. In *i2b2 workshop on challenges in natural language processing for clinical data*, pages 10–11. Citeseer.

Philipp Koehn. 2005. Europarl: A parallel corpus for statistical machine translation. In *MT summit*, volume 5, pages 79–86.

Guillaume Lample, Miguel Ballesteros, Sandeep Subramanian, Kazuya Kawakami, and Chris Dyer. 2016. Neural architectures for named entity recognition. *arXiv preprint arXiv:1603.01360*.

Todd Lingren, Louise Deleger, Katalin Molnar, Haijun Zhai, Jareen Meinzen-Derr, Megan Kaiser, Laura Stoutenborough, Qi Li, and Imre Solti. 2013. https://doi.org/10.1136/amiajnl-2013-001837 Evaluating the impact of pre-annotation on annotation speed and potential bias: Natural language processing gold standard development for clinical named entity recognition in clinical trial announcements. *Journal of the American Medical Informatics Association : JAMIA*, 21.

Tomas Mikolov, Ilya Sutskever, Kai Chen, Greg S Corrado, and Jeff Dean. 2013. http://papers.nips.cc/paper/5021-distributed-representations-of-words-and-phrases-and-their-compositionality.pdf Distributed representations of words and phrases and their compositionality. In C. J. C. Burges, L. Bottou, M. Welling, Z. Ghahramani, and K. Q. Weinberger, editors, *Advances in Neural Information Processing Systems 26*, pages 3111–3119. Curran Associates, Inc.

Ishna Neamatullah, Margaret M Douglass, H Lehman Li-wei, Andrew Reisner, Mauricio Villarroel, William J Long, Peter Szolovits, George B Moody, Roger G Mark, and Gari D Clifford. 2008. Automated de-identification of free-text medical records. *BMC medical informatics and decision making*, 8(1):32.

Naoaki Okazaki. 2007. http://www.chokkan.org/software/crfsuite/ Crfsuite: a fast implementation of conditional random fields (crfs).

Lance A Ramshaw and Mitchell P Marcus. 1999. Text chunking using transformation-based learning. In *Natural language processing using very large corpora*, pages 157–176. Springer.

Patrick Ruch, Robert H Baud, Anne-Marie Rassinoux, Pierrette Bouillon, and Gilbert Robert. 2000. Medical document anonymization with a semantic lexicon. In *Proceedings of the AMIA Symposium*, page 729. American Medical Informatics Association.

Erik F Sang and Fien De Meulder. 2003. Introduction to the conll-2003 shared task: Language-independent named entity recognition. *arXiv preprint cs/0306050*.

Jörg Tiedemann. 2016. Finding alternative translations in a large corpus of movie subtitle. In *LREC*.

Hui Yang and Jonathan M Garibaldi. 2015. Automatic detection of protected health information from clinic narratives. *Journal of biomedical informatics*, 58:S30–S38.

Augmenting a De-identification System for Swedish Clinical Text Using Open Resources and Deep Learning

Hanna Berg
Department of Computer
and Systems Sciences
Stockholm University
hanna.berg@dsv.su.se

Hercules Dalianis
Department of Computer
and Systems Sciences
Stockholm University
hercules@dsv.su.se

Abstract

Electronic patient records are produced in abundance every day and there is a demand to use them for research or management purposes. The records, however, contain information in the free text that can identify the patient and therefore tools are needed to identify this sensitive information.

The aim is to compare two machine learning algorithms, Long Short-Term Memory (LSTM) and Conditional Random Fields (CRF) applied to a Swedish clinical data set annotated for de-identification. The results show that CRF performs better than deep learning with LSTM, with CRF giving the best results with an F_1 score of 0.91 when adding more data from within the same domain. Adding general open data did, on the other hand, not improve the results.

1 Introduction

Electronic health records (EHR) are today produced in abundance and consist of information valuable to improve the medical care of future patients. They are, however, seldom reused for research as free text in patient records often contain possibly identifiable information about patients. To enable access to electronic health records while preserving patient privacy there is a need for automatic de-identification.

The US Health Insurance Portability and Accountability Act (HIPAA) defines 18 categories of Protected Health Information (PHI) which has to be concealed for EHRs to be considered de-identified in the US (Health Insurance Portability and Accountability Act (HIPAA), 2003). The categories include names, geographic divisions smaller than state, dates related to an individual, contact information and other data that can uniquely identify the individual.

Modules built to identify PHI, primarily rely on two methods: Rule-based methods and supervised machine-learning methods (Meystre et al., 2010). The two methods are often used together in hybrid systems (Stubbs et al., 2017). Rule-based methods do not require annotated data for training, are easy to modify and the results are easy to interpret, but they lack robustness and designing rules is a complex task (Meystre et al., 2010). Machine learning methods may provide greater robustness, but require an abundant amount of annotated data. According to Dernoncourt et al. (2017), statistical machine learning models require feature engineering, while artificial neural networks (ANN) does not. The latter does, however, require more data.

Lee et al. (2017) show that training a model on a large source dataset and then fine-tuning by retraining it on the smaller target data set can improve the results in comparison to only using the smallest data set. While the data sets used by Lee et al. (2017) consisted of 29,000 PHI instances in the smaller target data set and 61,000 PHI instances in the larger source data set the largest available Swedish data set, the Stockholm EPR PHI Corpus, has only 4,421 instances of PHI (Velupillai et al., 2009; Dalianis and Velupillai, 2010). It does exist a smaller related corpus with Electronic Health Records with annotations for de-identification, the Stockholm EPR PHI Domain Corpus (Henriksson et al., 2017b). For a larger data set with general Swedish text annotated for named entity recognition, Stockholm Umeå Corpus exists (Östling, 2012).

This study investigates the possibilities of augmenting the quality of de-identification by adding a general Swedish data set for named entity recognition such as Stockholm Umeå Corpus to already existing annotated PHI data sets and secondly the

Proceedings of the Workshop on NLP and Pseudonymisation, pages 8–15,
Turku, Finland, 30 September 2019. © 2019 Linköping University Electronic Press

use of deep learning methods such as LSTM.

2 Previous research

The state-of-the-art de-identification systems have for a long time been hybrid systems, where a machine learning approach, typically Conditional Random Fields (CRF) is used to identify classes including names, professions, and locations and a rule-based approach is used to identify rarely occurring or regular classes as zip codes, phone numbers and e-mail addresses (Uzuner et al., 2007; Stubbs et al., 2015). The best result during the i2b2 de-identification challenge 2014 (Stubbs et al., 2015) has a micro-averaged entity-based recall of 93.90%, a precision of 97.63% and an F_1 score of 0.96 on i2b2 PHI-categories.

The first neural network de-identification system was introduced in 2016 (Dernoncourt et al., 2017). This system used a type of deep learning with recurrent neural networks (RNN) called long short-term memory (LSTM) with three layers: A character enhanced token-embedding layer, a label prediction layer and a label sequence optimisation layer. The model is bidirectional to better handle long term dependencies. The ANN model presented, performed better than the best system from the i2b2 2014 challenge. Combining Bi-LSTM and CRF further improved the system. Similar systems based on LSTM and CRF have been successful for de-identification (Liu et al., 2017), and during the i2b2 de-identification challenge of 2016 a model combining an LSTM, a CRF and rules won the challenge with an entity-based micro-averaged F_1 score of 0.91 for HIPAA classes (Stubbs et al., 2017).

The largest Swedish dataset with health records annotated for de-identification is the Stockholm EPR PHI Corpus, which is a part of Health Bank - Swedish Health Record Research Bank. Health Bank encompasses structured and unstructured data from 512 clinical units from Karolinska University Hospital collected from 2006 to 2014 (Dalianis et al., 2015).

The first results for identifying PHI based on the gold standard of the Stockholm EPR PHI Corpus can be seen in Table 1. De-identification tasks based on CRF as well as rules have been carried out on this data set with precision scores between 85% and 92.65%, recall scores between 71% and 81% and F_1 scores between 0.76 and 0.87 (Dalianis and Velupillai, 2010; Henriksson et al., 2017b; Dalianis and Boström, 2012; Boström and Dalianis, 2012). The best de-identification system based on the corpus was developed by Henriksson et al. (2017b), using token, lemma, part of speech, capitalisation, digit, compounds, and dictionary matches against the medical terminologies SNOMED CT, MeSH as features. Predictive performance estimates yielded an F_1 score of 0.87.

McMurry et al. (2013) have trained decision tree classifiers using 28 features based on part of speech tags, term frequencies, and dictionaries in open journal publications and confidential physician notes to recognise non-PHI words. According to the study, distributional differences between private and open medical texts can be used to classify PHI.

3 Data and method

3.1 Data

Three data sets for de-identification are used: The Stockholm EPR PHI Corpus, the Stockholm EPR PHI Domain Corpus and Stockholm Umeå Corpus 3.0 (SUC). The data consists of both clinical data[1] and open-source data. The Stockholm EPR PHI Corpus is used both for development, training, and testing, while Stockholm EPR PHI Domain Corpus and SUC are only used for training.

All data is encoded using BIOES-encoding, indicating the position of the token within the PHI entity. It encoded whether the token was in the **B**eginning, **I**nside or **E**nding of a multi-token entity, a **S**ingle entity or **O**utside an entity (Reimers and Gurevych, 2017).

Stockholm EPR PHI Corpus consists of 100 patient records from five clinical units: Neurology, orthopaedia, infection, dental surgery and nutrition at Karolinska University Hospital (Dalianis and Velupillai, 2010) and has approximately 200,000 tokens. The Stockholm EPR PHI Corpus was first manually annotated by three annotators into 28 PHI classes based on HIPAA and enriched with further classes (Velupillai et al., 2009). The annotations were later on merged into conceptually similar classes while removing classes with few instances, creating a gold standard with eight PHI annotation classes: *Age, numeric and non-numeric full dates and*

[1] This research has been approved by the Regional Ethical Review Board in Stockholm (2012/834-31/5).

Class	Annotated	Retrieved	Relevant	Exact matches Precision	Recall	F-score	Partial matches Precision	Recall	F-score
Age	56	45	37	0.822222	0.660714	0.732673	0.904762	0.778061	0.836642
Date_Part	710	654	617	0.943425	0.869014	0.904692	0.946196	0.871730	0.907438
Full_Date	500	426	342	0.802817	0.684000	0.738661	**0.931665**	**0.802106**	**0.862045**
First_Name	923	749	713	0.951936	0.772481	0.852871	0.954606	0.773772	0.854729
Last_Name	928	816	777	**0.952206**	**0.837284**	**0.891055**	0.961653	0.845484	0.899835
Health_Care_Unit	1021	689	559	0.811321	0.547502	0.653801	0.921497	0.608116	0.732705
Location	148	73	54	0.739726	0.364865	0.488688	0.778539	0.379129	0.509933
Phone_Number	135	86	80	0.930233	0.592593	0.723982	0.954195	0.613105	0.746535
Total	4421	3538	3179	0.898530	0.719068	0.798844	0.941190	0.751441	0.835680

Additional file 5 (Table S5) - Results of the manual Consensus Gold standard using ten-fold cross-evaluation

Table 1: Results from Dalianis and Velupillai (2010)

date parts, first names, last names, health care units, locations, and *phone numbers* (Dalianis and Velupillai, 2010). Locations include not only places but also companies. Health care units were only annotated as Health Care Unit if they were considered identifiable by the annotator. The distribution of PHI is presented in Table 2.

Stockholm EPR PHI Domain Corpus consists of data from three clinical units: Geriatric, oncology and orthopaedic at Karolinska University Hospital. It has approximately 116,000 tokens. It uses the same eight annotation classes as the Stockholm EPR PHI Corpus. In the original version, almost half of the corpus is annotated, while the other half is not. The original annotation for health care unit followed other guidelines than the one set in (Dalianis and Velupillai, 2010). The Health Care Unit annotations and other half of the corpus were therefore re-annotated in this study. Health care units were only annotated if they were identifiable within the Stockholm area.

Stockholm Umeå Corpus 3.0 consists of Swedish texts from press, scientific writing and prose collected during the 1990s and has over one million tokens (Östling, 2012; Gustafson-Capková and Hartmann, 2006). The latest release was SUC 3.0, released in 2012. The corpus is annotated with part-of-speech tags, morphological analysis, lemma as well as ten named-entity classes. The used classes are *person, place, institution, animal, myth*[2], *product, work, measurements (with age as a subclass), event* and *other*. The annotations for person, location and age were used in this study, further the person annotation was semi-manually divided into first names and last names. The entire corpus is used.

	EPR	Domain	SUC
First Name	928	380	11,748
Last Name	923	524	9,402
Phone Number	135	47	0
Age	56	52	427
Full Date	500	382	0
Date Part	710	555	0
Health Care Unit	1,021	387	24
Location	148	96	9,388
Total	4,421	2,886	30,989

Table 2: Overview of annotated Protected Health Information entities. Note that Date Parts, Full Dates or Phone Numbers are not annotated in SUC.

The Stockholm EPR PHI Corpus was first divided into two sets: One small for development and validation with 10% of the patient records and one for training and testing by cross-validation with 90% of the patient records. For the CRF, tenfold cross-validation was used. The patient records from the Stockholm EPR PHI Corpus were divided into ten folds. The Stockholm EPR Domain Corpus and SUC Corpus were divided into ten folds, where for each fold 90% of the sentences were used for training. Only the folds from the Stockholm EPR PHI Corpus were used for testing. A similar approach was done for LSTM,

[2]The myth annotation consists of names of mythical creates and places and the animal annotation consists of names of animals.

but used validation data for early stopping. The LSTM has only been evaluated on the three first folds due to time constraints.

3.2 Method

This study compares the predictive powers for three models based on the data described above. The first model is only trained on data from the Stockholm EPR PHI Corpus, the second model is trained on data from the Stockholm EPR PHI Corpus and the Stockholm EPR Domain Corpus. The last model is trained on the Stockholm EPR PHI Corpus and SUC. All models are evaluated on data from the Stockholm EPR PHI Corpus using ten cross fold-validation.

The result is evaluated with micro averaged entity-based precision, recall and F_1 score, which is the standard for evaluating named entity recognition (Stubbs et al., 2015).

3.2.1 LSTM

Recurrent neural network (RRN) is a type of deep learning artificial neural network designed for processing sequential data (Dernoncourt et al., 2017). The bidirectional LSTM architecture is designed to access long-range dependencies in both forward and backward directions (Dernoncourt et al., 2017). The experiment uses the architecture described in Lample et al. (2016) based on an open-source implementation with Tensorflow[3].

As stated by Lample et al. (2016), character-based representations can be used to capture both morphological and orthographic information. The character-representations are learned from the used training set for each experiment. Pre-trained word representation is used, based on a subset of clinical text from Health Bank of 200 millions tokens producing 300,824 vectors with a dimension of 300.

The implementation uses the adaptive learning rate method *Adam*, an algorithm for optimisation of stochastic objective functions (Kingma and Ba, 2014). It computes different learning rates for each parameter based on estimates from the first and second moments of the gradients. The *learning rate* was set to 0.001 with a *decay of 0.9*.

Dropout was used with a *dropout rate of 0.5*. This was used with a *batch size of 64*. The training is done in a maximum of *20 epochs*, with early stopping if no improvement three times in a row in the development set. The model was then evaluated on the test set. The CRF layer (Lample et al., 2016) was not used as it did not show any benefits for the validation set compared to using only LSTM.

3.2.2 CRF

Conditional Random Fields (CRFs) with linear chain is a statistical machine learning method first introduced by Lafferty et al. (2001) that predicts sequences of labels based on sequences in the input. A set of features is typically defined to extract features for each word in a sentence. The CRF tries to determine weights that will maximise the likelihood of leading to the labels in the training data.

In this study, CRFSuite (Okazaki, 2007) is used with a the sklearn-crfsuite wrapper[4]. The features used are: Word as lower case, the first and last four and eight letters, lemma, part of speech tag, if the word is in lower case, upper case or title case, if there are only numbers in the word or only letters in the word or if it has special characters, how many letters, numbers or other characters the word has. This is carried out with a window size of 5. Information about which heading a word comes from is included for texts from the Stockholm EPR PHI Corpus. Furthermore, the CRF uses gazetteers for first names, last names, locations, honorifics or medical profession titles, hospitals in the Stockholm region and regular expressions for identifying date parts, full dates and telephone numbers.

The CRF uses gradient descent with Limited-memory BFGS (L-BFGS) for optimization. LBFGS is an optimization algorithm (Koller et al., 2007).

Lemma and part of speech tagging for each word was performed with Stagger (Östling, 2012) for the Stockholm EPR PHI Corpus and the Stockholm EPR Domain Corpus. SUC is already manually annotated with lemma and part of speech.

4 Results

4.1 LSTM - Results

As seen in Table 3 presenting the results for the LSTM, the systems handle first names, last names, date parts, full dates better than ages, health care units and location.

[3]https://github.com/guillaumegenthial/sequence_tagging

[4]https://sklearn-crfsuite.readthedocs.io

	EPR PHI			EPR PHI + Domain			EPR PHI + SUC		
	P %	R %	F_1	P %	R %	F_1	P %	R %	F_1
First Name	93.79	92.63	0.93	95.16	93.99	**0.95**	92.46	91.46	0.92
Last Name	93.09	94.87	0.94	97.19	95.11	**0.96**	90.77	96.68	0.94
Phone Number	96.30	94.44	**0.95**	90.00	95.83	0.93	95.24	91.67	0.93
Age	80.56	75.56	0.78	70.00	75.56	0.72	91.67	75.56	**0.82**
Full Date	91.38	96.46	0.94	91.98	95.77	0.94	92.59	95.82	0.94
Date Part	95.6	97.96	**0.97**	93.51	97.24	0.95	93.37	94.60	0.94
Health Care Unit	61.19	69.20	**0.65**	58.95	54.70	0.57	59.06	51.88	0.55
Location	76.90	75.27	**0.76**	69.87	70.15	0.69	61.55	86.54	0.70
Overall	85.87	88.96	**0.87**	86.28	85.46	0.86	84.78	85.44	0.85

Table 3: Entity-based evaluation for LSTM for the first three folds. The mean is presented for each label. The highest F_1 scores are highlighted for each class.

The only two types of PHI improved when adding SUC is *age* and *full date* and no improvements can be seen in any other classes. Rather a drop of performance can be seen for location, last names and first names. There is a small increase of recall for first names and locations, but with lower precision.

Stockholm EPR PHI Corpus alone performs considerably better for identifying phone numbers, locations and health care units, while first names and full dates seem to be identified correctly to a greater extent with additional data from the Stockholm EPR PHI Domain Corpus.

Overall, there is no improvement when adding another corpus to the training, but rather a drop in performance.

4.2 CRF - Results

Overall the CRF systems perform well, particularly for finding dates and names. The recall is lower for *Phone Number* and both the precision and recall is lower for *Health Care Unit, Location* and *Age*. As seen in Table 4 with results for the CRF, compared to LSTM results in Table 3, the CRF performs better overall with greater precision, but the LSTM has a higher recall.

Adding the Domain Data increases the F_1 score marginally. Some small, likely insignificant, improvements can be seen for *Health Care Unit, Age* and *Phone Number*. There is not the same drop of performance as for the LSTM systems.

Adding SUC does not improve the ability to predict, and instead both precision and recall is lower for all classes except last names and ages. The drop of performance is however less severe than for the LSTM.

5 Analysis

Health Care Unit and *Location* are the most commingled PHI classes. Health care units are often named by their geographic location. *Huddinge* can for example refer to the hospital *Karolinska University Hospital Huddinge* but also the municipality *Huddinge*. In the gold standard, locations are annotated as a part of the health care unit occasionally depending if it is an actual part of the name and whether it is directly adjacent to an identifiable health care unit. Errors are partly caused by the difficulty to distinguish these cases. Furthermore, some health care units are only occasionally annotated as PHI, which also makes it more difficult for the system to learn the structure. *ASIH*, which stands for Advanced Care At Home in Swedish, is for example in 8 of 20 cases annotated as a singular health care unit entity.

Location is a class with generally low F_1 score. One reason for this may be that the test data includes companies as locations. Location has relatively few annotations, and almost one-quarter of these are company annotations. Companies are overall rarely occurring, but frequently mentioned in one patient record. In the record with the most company annotations, none of the seven mentioned companies is found by any system.

When identifying age, the numeral in the age entity is often correctly identified, but the upcoming word is either incorrectly included or missed. The unit following the numeral, often 'years', is occasionally annotated within the PHI and occasionally not, which is one reason for these errors. Age annotations where the numeral is followed by 'årig' (year-old) are found to a greater extent than those followed by 'år' (years).

	EPR PHI			EPR PHI + Domain			EPR PHI + SUC		
	P %	R %	F_1	P %	R %	F_1	P %	R %	F_1
First Name	95.05	92.78	**0.94**	95.50	91.41	0.93	94.51	92.24	0.93
Last Name	97.02	92.20	0.94	96.39	90.36	0.93	96.93	0.93	**0.95**
Phone Number	92.81	81.52	0.87	94.58	84.32	**0.89**	96.14	72.14	0.82
Age	79.29	60.95	0.68	85.09	71.27	0.77	89.67	76.21	**0.82**
Full Date	98.62	99.15	**0.99**	96.34	94.74	0.96	95.82	93.28	0.94
Date Part	97.06	95.68	**0.96**	97.45	94.73	**0.96**	95.46	90.08	0.93
Health Care Unit	86.11	66.40	0.75	88.62	72.79	**0.80**	85.45	67.38	0.75
Location	74.07	73.70	**0.72**	76.05	59.89	0.66	62.40	70.92	0.65
Overall	93.76	86.53	0.90	94.66	86.72	**0.91**	92.31	84.97	0.88

Table 4: Entity-based evaluation for CRF with tenfold cross-validation. The mean is presented for each label. The highest F_1 scores are highlighted for each class.

Uncommon names, common words that are also names, misspelt names and names in lower case are less often identified. This especially happens in contexts where there are no other words, either to the left or right. This is common in sections similar to 'Assigned nurse'. There are some cases where first names are annotated as last names and vice verse. The first names *Carina, Riita* and *Abdul* are annotated as last names in the gold standard, leading to errors.

Non-PHI adjacent to a PHI entity is annotated as PHI and more general entities, similar to annotated PHI, for example "the summer of 2007", are more often mistaken as PHI. There are also some cases where inconsistent annotation leads to false positives for especially Health Care Units, they also lead to false negatives. The systems also manage to find some PHI not previously annotated in the gold standard.

6 Discussion

In comparison to other work where the Stockholm EPR PHI Corpus is used to classify PHI this set of features and CRF implementation works well for identifying PHI. The CRF also performed better by itself than the LSTM when focusing on the overall F_1 score. This the highest recall overall of 88.96% is nonetheless achieved with the LSTM system and without any additional corpus.

There is an overall drop of recall and F_1 when adding other corpora to the LSTM version, while the CRF version is slightly improved by adding the EPR PHI Domain corpus, with an F_1 score of 0.91. On the other hand the highest recall for *Last name* is achieved using LSTM and SUC and the recall of *First name* and *Last Name* is also improved with additional EPR data in. It could be argued that recall is more important than precision and and that *Last name* and *First name* are two of the most sensitive classes.

In SUC, organisations and places are annotated separately. Company names tend to sound like names and occur in similar contexts like health care units. A distinction between locations and companies may enable the usage of the organisation annotation from SUC, with possible improvements on similar labels as well as reduce the heterogeneity.

Differences between the annotation quality or guidelines may also affect the result. Inaccuracies within the Stockholm EPR PHI Corpus is mentioned in the analysis. The Stockholm EPR PHI Corpus was annotated by three annotators and further examined by others. The Stockholm EPR Domain Corpus was, however, originally annotated by only one person and re-annotated for this study by one of the authors to comply with the annotation guidelines of the Stockholm EPR PHI Corpus. This corpus is likely to have more inaccuracies than the Stockholm EPR PHI Corpus.

There is generally a drop in performance between domains and within cross clinical or cross hospital settings. Therefore, it may not come as a surprise that training partially on another domain does not benefit the classifier regardless of the data size. Open text within the medical domain may be more beneficial due to higher domain similarities. A selection of specific documents within SUC is unlikely to benefit the classifier as only a minority of SUC includes medical text.

Using partial match may improve the results for multi-token entity expressions, such as phone numbers, locations, dates and health care units, see Figure 1.

7 Conclusion and future directions

This study aimed to investigate the possibilities of augmenting the quality of de-identification by using annotated data sets for named entities or the use of deep learning methods such as LSTM. The findings suggest that adding data from a general corpus for named entities is not a viable option, but perhaps for individual classes. LSTM performs reasonably well by itself, even if the CRF models seem to perform better. It is worth noting that the LSTM is not yet evaluated on all folds, and considering the increase of recall, it is still warranted to see if a hybrid version of this CRF and LSTM can improve the results further. One possible approach would be to use a LSTM system to de-identify personal names and a CRF system to de-identify phone numbers, locations, dates and health care units.

The current study only examined the effects of using two corpora together as training data, and not the performance when training on one data set, the Stockholm EPR PHI Corpus or SUC, and then using domain adaptation to the target date set, the Stockholm EPR PHI Corpus. While the identification of some PHI classes benefit from added data, there are also classes where no improvements are seen despite data being added.

The analysis has shown that there is a need to revise the old gold standard for the Stockholm EPR PHI by adding previously overlooked PHI, changing PHI accidentally annotated as another PHI, and possibly review the guidelines for the manual annotation of health care units, locations and ages.

Our best performing de-identification system surpasses previous systems based on Stockholm EPR PHI Corpus. It performs in line with the best performing de-identification systems from the latest i2b2 de-identification challenge (Stubbs et al., 2017) but lower than the best from earlier challenge (Stubbs et al., 2015). One observation, however, is that data set in Stubbs et al. (2015) is seven times larger than the Stockholm EPR PHI Corpus in terms of both tokens and PHI instances (Dernoncourt et al., 2017).

Acknowledgments

We are grateful to the DataLEASH project for funding this research work.

References

Henrik Boström and Hercules Dalianis. 2012. De-identifying health records by means of active learning. In *Proceedings of ICML 2012, The 29th International Conference on Machine Learning*, pages 1–3.

Hercules Dalianis and Henrik Boström. 2012. Releasing a Swedish clinical corpus after removing all words–de-identification experiments with conditional random fields and random forests. In *Proceedings of the Third Workshop on Building and Evaluating Resources for Biomedical Text Mining (BioTxtM 2012) held in conjunction with LREC*, pages 45–48.

Hercules Dalianis, Aron Henriksson, Maria Kvist, Sumithra Velupillai, and Rebecka Weegar. 2015. HEALTH BANK–A Workbench for Data Science Applications in Healthcare. In *Proceedings of the CAiSE-2015 Industry Track co-located with 27th Conference on Advanced Information Systems Engineering (CAiSE 2015), J. Krogstie, G. Juel-Skielse and V. Kabilan, (Eds.), Stockholm, Sweden, June 11, 2015, CEUR, Vol-1381*, pages 1–18.

Hercules Dalianis and Sumithra Velupillai. 2010. De-identifying Swedish clinical text - Refinement of a Gold Standard and Experiments with Conditional Random fields. *Journal of Biomedical Semantics*, 1:6.

Franck Dernoncourt, Ji Young Lee, Ozlem Uzuner, and Peter Szolovits. 2017. De-identification of patient notes with recurrent neural networks. *Journal of the American Medical Informatics Association*, 24(3):596–606.

Sofia Gustafson-Capková and Britt Hartmann. 2006. Manual of the Stockholm Umeå Corpus version 2.0. *https://spraakbanken.gu.se/parole/Docs/SUC2.0-manual.pdf.*

Health Insurance Portability and Accountability Act (HIPAA). 2003. http://www.cdc.gov/mmwr/preview/mmwrhtml/m2e411a1.htm U.S. Department of Health and Human Services. Accessed 2019-06-17.

Aron Henriksson, Maria Kvist, and Hercules Dalianis. 2017b. Detecting Protected Health Information in Heterogeneous Clinical Notes. volume 245, pages 393–397.

Diederik P Kingma and Jimmy Ba. 2014. Adam: A method for stochastic optimization. *arXiv preprint arXiv:1412.6980.*

Daphne Koller, Nir Friedman, Sašo Džeroski, Charles Sutton, Andrew McCallum, Avi Pfeffer, Pieter Abbeel, Ming-Fai Wong, David Heckerman, Chris Meek, et al. 2007. *Introduction to statistical relational learning*. MIT press.

John Lafferty, Andrew McCallum, and Fernando Pereira. 2001. Conditional random fields: Probabilistic models for segmenting and labeling sequence data. In *Proceedings 18th International Conference on Machine Learning*, pages 282–289. Morgan Kaufmann.

Guillaume Lample, Miguel Ballesteros, Sandeep Subramanian, Kazuya Kawakami, and Chris Dyer. 2016. Neural architectures for named entity recognition. *arXiv preprint arXiv:1603.01360*.

Ji Young Lee, Franck Dernoncourt, and Peter Szolovits. 2017. Transfer learning for named-entity recognition with neural networks. *arXiv preprint arXiv:1705.06273*.

Zengjian Liu, Buzhou Tang, Xiaolong Wang, and Qingcai Chen. 2017. De-identification of clinical notes via recurrent neural network and conditional random field. *Journal of biomedical informatics*, 75:S34–S42.

Andrew J. McMurry, Britt Fitch, Guergana Savova, Isaac S. Kohane, and Ben Y. Reis. 2013. https://doi.org/10.1186/1472-6947-13-112 Improved de-identification of physician notes through integrative modeling of both public and private medical text. *BMC medical informatics and decision making*, 13:112–112. 24083569[pmid].

Stephane Meystre, Jeffrey Friedlin, Brett South, Shuying Shen, and Matthew Samore. 2010. Automatic de-identification of textual documents in the electronic health record: a review of recent research. *BMC Medical Research Methodology*, 10(1):70.

Naoaki Okazaki. 2007. http://www.chokkan.org/software/crfsuite CRFsuite: a fast implementation of Conditional Random Fields. Accessed 2019-06-17.

Robert Östling. 2012. Stagger: A modern POS tagger for Swedish. In *The Fourth Swedish Language Technology Conference, Lund, Sweden*.

Nils Reimers and Iryna Gurevych. 2017. Optimal hyperparameters for deep lstm-networks for sequence labeling tasks. *arXiv preprint arXiv:1707.06799*.

Amber Stubbs, Michele Filannino, and Özlem Uzuner. 2017. De-identification of psychiatric intake records: Overview of 2016 cegs n-grid shared tasks track 1. *Journal of biomedical informatics*, 75:S4–S18.

Amber Stubbs, Christopher Kotfila, and Özlem Uzuner. 2015. Automated systems for the de-identification of longitudinal clinical narratives: Overview of 2014 i2b2/uthealth shared task track 1. *Journal of biomedical informatics*, 58:S11–S19.

Özlem Uzuner, Yuan Luo, and Peter Szolovits. 2007. Evaluating the State-of-the-Art in Automatic De-identification. *Journal of the American Medical Informatics Association*, 14(5):550–563.

Sumithra Velupillai, Hercules Dalianis, Martin Hassel, and Gunnar H Nilsson. 2009. Developing a standard for de-identifying electronic patient records written in Swedish: precision, recall and F-measure in a manual and computerized annotation trial. *International Journal of Medical Informatics*, 78(12):e19–e26.

Pseudonymisation of Swedish Electronic Patient Records Using a Rule-based Approach

Hercules Dalianis
Department of Computer
and Systems Sciences
Stockholm University
hercules@dsv.su.se

Abstract

This study describes a rule-based pseudonymisation system for Swedish clinical text and its evaluation. The pseudonymisation system replaces already tagged Protected Health Information (PHI) with realistic surrogates. There are eight types of manually annotated PHIs in the electronic patient records; personal first and last names, phone numbers, locations, dates, ages and healthcare units.

Two evaluators, both computer scientists, one junior and one senior, evaluated whether a set of 98 electronic patients records where pseudonymised or not. Only 3.5 percent of the records were correctly judged as pseudonymised and 1.5 percent of the real ones were wrongly judged as pseudo, giving that in average 91 percent of the pseudonymised records were judged as real.

1 Introduction

Electronic patient records also called clinical text contain valuable information that may be extracted and used for improving healthcare, see Chapter 10 in (Dalianis, 2018).

The records are becoming more and more accessible for the research community, but under strict confidential restrictions since they contain sensitive information about patients. Before being accessible for research the electronic patient records are required to be anonymised in the way that they do not contain any information (or data tables) that may identify any patient. However in the unstructured part of the records, that is the free text fields, there is information such as personal names, phone numbers that may identify the patient. In the structured part there might also be sensitive information, but that is easily identifiable, since that column can be called social security number, temperature, or ICD-10-code.

Therefore, there is a significant research area in clinical text mining called automatic de-identification (DEID) of electronic patient records (Meystre et al., 2010; Uzuner et al., 2007). These DEID systems are either rule-based, machine learning-based or hybrid approaches where the best systems obtain up to 0.97 F-score, (Uzuner et al., 2007).

Of course, one requirement on these DEID systems is high recall over high precision since it is more important to find all instances of sensitive information than to risk predicting false positives.

A DEID system works in such a way that it tags the identified sensitive information or what more precisely is called Protected Health Information (PHI) and removes the sensitive information inside the PHI tag. The tag is left telling what type of PHI it contained. When the system misses identifying an entity in the text, such as a personal name or a phone number, it is visible and obvious. These un-identified PHIs are also called residual identifiers. One method to increase security is described by Carrell et al. (2013) and is called Hiding In Plain Sight (HIPS) and consists of replacing all the identified PHI tags with surrogates or pseudonymised information, such that the un-identified residual PHI will be perceived by the reader to be already replaced by a surrogate and hence pseudonymised. Pseudonymisation is the method where an identified PHI, for example, a personal first name is replaced with a fake first name, that obviously need to be a common name to diminish the risk of identification.

An example of a pseudonymised electronic patient record is presented in Figure 1.

A hypothesis is that when reading the patient records, the reader should not be annoyed by strange names or places or tags and focus on the

Proceedings of the Workshop on NLP and Pseudonymisation, pages 16–23,
Turku, Finland, 30 September 2019. © 2019 Linköping University Electronic Press

medical content.

The research question is whether a reader of an electronic patient record could reveal if one record as pseudonymised or not. The reader/evaluator should judge whether a clinical text describing a patient's personal name, family relation and mentioned addresses, phone numbers, locations, health care units and dates look real or not.

2 Related research

One of the first attempt in creating surrogates after the DEID process was presented by Sweeney (1996). Dates were replaced with a similar date nearby. Personal names were replaced with a fictitious unique name that sounded reasonable. The article does not mention how the system processed locations and phone numbers and other PHI.

In (Douglass et al., 2004), a similar approach is described where dates were shifted by the same random number of weeks or years, but keeping the days of the week. Personal names were replaced with names from a publicly available list from the Boston area in the US, but randomly mixing first and last names. Locations were replaced with randomly selected small towns. Hospital and clinical units were given fictitious names.

One of the first studies on Swedish was presented in (Alfalahi et al., 2012) and were carried out on the Stockholm EPR PHI Corpus (Velupillai et al., 2009), where personal names were replaced in a context-sensitive way. Female first names where replaced by common female first names, and similar for male names and for last names that also were replaced with common names. Gender-neutral first names are replaced with other randomly chosen gender-neutral name. Addresses and phone numbers are replaced, and dates are shifted, ages changed slightly. Locations and healthcare units are replaced with only one location and healthcare unit respectively.

Another study on the same Swedish corpus was carried out by Antfolk and Branting (2016). However the study focused only on locations. The system replaced locations such as *places, cities*, and *countries* with locations that were situated closely geographically. One problem was that many locations were misspellt or abbreviated and hence challenging to replace with a proper surrogate location. Prepositions in front of countries could pose problems since countries written in Swedish need the Swedish preposition *i* (English: in) while countries on islands require *på* (English: on). Complete addresses with street and number or cities were not replaced since they were not in the scope of the study.

Björkegren (2016) carried out a similar study on the same Swedish corpus and with focus on locations. The annotated class *Location* is a broad concept covering everything from a street, a place, a city, a municipality (Swe: kommun), a county, a country or a continent and sometimes an organisation, a company or a product name and thus difficult to process unless identifying what type of concept it is. The reason for this broad coverage is that the corpus was used for machine learning training and there were very few concepts for location in the corpus, hence several classes describing locations were collapsed into one class *Location* in the gold standard (Dalianis and Velupillai, 2010).

In the study by Björkegren (2016), an evaluation was carried out were three respondents had to evaluate which of the 17 patient records were pseudonymised and which contained real PHI. Half of the records were identified as pseudonymised thus indicating that the pseudonymisation program was not good enough. Many errors occurred in the geographical context where one street was mentioned in the wrong part of the city.

In another approach for English by Deleger et al. (2014), both the American English clinical corpus from Physionet, i2b2 and the Cincinnati Children's Hospital Medical Center (CCHMC) corpus were used. One important feature was when replacing one PHI in the data set it should not resemble any other replaced PHI. Personal names are replaced from a list of real names from US Census Bureau having a frequency above 144, meaning 0.004 percent of the data. Gender of personal names are replaced consistently. Combinations of street and street numbers are not reoccurring as in the original corpus. Email addresses are replaced with a set of a random set of characters as the length in the original email address.

Meystre et al. (2014) carried out a study where 86 patient records in English were de-identified and where none of the five treating physicians could recognise their patients after de-identification.

Grouin et al. (2015) carried out an experiment where they de-identified a group of patient records in French and they asked physicians to identify the patient. However, they could not succeed in this, unless they had access to the whole hospital system and found other documents of the same (de-identified) patient, so they could group and regroup patients and consequently identify them.

3 Methods and data

The method chosen for this study is rule-based since training data is scarce in the clinical domain that can be used for replacing sensitive PHI with realistic surrogates.

The implementation is carried out in the programming language Python. Three personal name lists are used representing Swedish female first names, male first names and last names, also lists with candidate surrogates in form of the 100 most common (frequent) Swedish personal names were prepared: female first and male first names and last names (gender-neutral), moreover, a list of all streets and place names in the city of Stockholm and locations in Sweden.

A list of all postal codes in Sweden, (where the 461 most common are used for candidate surrogates), a list of all area codes for phone numbers as well as a list of all prefixes for mobile phone numbers in Sweden and finally a list of generic candidate healthcare units were also used. These lists were also used by Velupillai et al. (2009) to build a de-identification system and re-used in this study for the rule-based psuedonymisation system.

The authors of the article (Antfolk and Branting, 2016) kindly provided a hierarchical list with locations. Locations divided into the different Swedish counties and finally all locations in the world including islands in all continents of the world and capital cities except the locations in Sweden.

Special list for town squares and parks were provided by Andreas Amsenius that had used them for earlier work on de-identifications of emails in Swedish.

For an overview of all lists and number of entities, see Table 1.

The used data consists of the Stockholm EPR PHI Corpus[1] that contains 100 electronic patient records written in Swedish from five different clinical units: *neurology, orthopaedia, infection, dental surgery* and *nutrition* (Velupillai et al., 2009; Dalianis and Velupillai, 2010), see Table 2 for the distribution of the eight types of PHI entities. The Stockholm EPR PHI Corpus is part of Health Bank - Swedish Health Record Research Bank.

The pseudonymisation program work in such a way that it matches the found tagged personal first name and last name. The first name is checked whether the name is in the list of male first names or female first names. If it is a male name, it is replaced with another common male name and if it is a female name, it is replaced with another com-

Swedish entities	**Number**	**Most common**
Female first names	122,622	100
Male first names	120,167	100
Gender-neutral names	22	22
Last names	34,894	100
Health care units	430	20
Postal codes	9,724	461
Streets in Stockholm	1,719	-
Parks in Stockholm	131	-
Provinces (Landskap)	21	-
Places in provinces	27,883	-
Squares and places	6,910	-
Area code phone numbers	265	-
Prefix mobile phone numbers	17	-
Outside Sweden		
Continents	5	-
Countries	203	-
Capitals	206	-
Cities	1,386	-
Provinces	131	-

Table 1: Overview of all the types of lists used both to find PHIs and also to generate surrogates (Column most common). Observe that Provinces and Continents are hierarchical in one level; hence Provinces and Continents are not replaced, just the content within each group.

[1]This research has been approved by the Regional Ethical Review Board in Stockholm (2012/834-31/5).

mon female name. First names are also replaced in such a way that if it is repeated several times in a paragraph, then the same generated pseudonym is kept. If the first name is not in any female or male name list it is spellchecked using a Levenshtein spell checking module implemented by Nick Sweeting in 2014[2] based on Peter Norvig's spell checker, but here in this study adapted for personal name correction, first using a male personal name dictionary and then a female name dictionary. Gender-neutral names are replaced with a gender neutral name, and also genitive "s" in names is always taken care of. For last names they are replaced with one common last name, no spell checking is used.

Street addresses are replaced with another random street address in Stockholm with a random street number, ditto postal number, and postal location. Locations outside of Stockholm are replaced according to a system that if a location in a specific county is found, it is replaced with another random location on the same county for geographical proximity, and when the county name itself is found it is not replaced since counties are considered as large geographical areas. The same goes for continents, a country in one continent is replaced with another random country but not the continent name itself.

Dates are shifted plus seven days upwards or downwards. Weekdays and weekends are kept intact, since the activities on clinical units are different on weekdays compared to weekends.

Ages are shifted a couple of years upwards or downwards.

Regarding phone numbers, the area code for fixed phone numbers are randomly shifted to another area code for fixed phone numbers as well as the whole number were randomly changed. For mobile phone numbers, the same procedure is carried out but where the prefix for mobile phone numbers is randomly shifted to another prefix for mobile phone numbers.

For healthcare units, they are randomly changed to some few generic healthcare units that cannot identify a specific healthcare unit, see also Table 1.

Any found social security number if found is simply removed.

The data to be evaluated were prepared as follows: The texts were randomly pseudonymised so half of the 98 record text were pseudonymised and the other half were real non-pseudonymised patient records. The random distribution became 58 true records and 40 pseudo records, hence 59 percent true records and 41 percent pseudo records, which as the result of the *random.choice()* function of Python.

To avoid forcing the evaluators to read texts with few or no PHIs the data were prepared in the following way: First by ordering the 98 records with the highest amount of PHIs first and with falling density and then by extracting a section of maximum 20 consecutive lines with the highest density of PHI. Before presenting the records to the evaluators, the tags marking up the PHI were removed.

The reason to give the evaluators only 20 consecutive lines with the highest density of PHI was to make the evaluation practical otherwise the evaluators had to read plenty of clinical text (with no PHIs) and the evaluation would take long time be tedious and tiresome for the evaluator, and risk that the will not be concentrated on their work.

4 Results

The pseudonymisation program was executed on the whole Stockholm EPR PHI Corpus that contained the tags described in Table 2. In the figure, the number of replacements by the pseudonymisation program is also presented.

In Figure 1, a original but pseudonymised record can be seen, where first and last personal names have been replaced as well as healthcare units and phone numbers.

5 Evaluation

The evaluation of the system was carried out by two evaluators, both computer scientists one senior and one junior with knowledge in clinical data mining. The senior computer scientist is a second language Swedish speaker, and the junior computer scientist is a native speaker of Swedish. None of the evaluators had seen the electronic patient records beforehand. Both evaluators had also signed confidentiality agreements, the same as the author of this article had signed.

The two evaluators, the senior and the junior, could only correctly judge that 4 and 6 records respectively were pseudonymised of the total 98 records where 40 were pseudo records.

[2]Nick Sweeting 2014 implementation of Peter Norvig's spell checker, https://github.com/pirate/spellchecker/

Epikris Huddinge
Ansv. specialist-/ överläkare Caroline Berg
Journalförare Marianne Lindgren
Utskriftsdatum 20120325
Vårdtid 20120311-20120318
Huvuddiagnos enl. ICD-10
Anamnes 52-årig kvinna, välkänd på kliniken. Går hos Karin Lundgren samt på smärtmottagningen.
Har en kronisk huvudvärk utan säker genes. Insatt på Metadon, Actiqe och Stesolid.
Sökte den 22/5 pga ohållbar situation med bristfällig smärtkontroll.
Pat är frusterad över lång väntetid på inneliggande utsättning av opiater
som skulle göras via IVA och planerats av dr Torbjörn Andreasson.
Pat kommer till NIVA och kräver att få läggas in på IVA och hotar att sluta med samtliga mediciner.
Pat har haft flera samtal med PAL på Löwet, Sandra Månsson. Hänvisar till tidigare anteckningar.

In Eng:
Discharge letter Huddinge
Responsible. specialist / chief physician Caroline Berg
Medical secretary Marianne Lindgren
Print Date 20120325
Care episode 20120311-20120318
Main diagnosis according to ICD-10
History of 52-year-old woman, well known in the clinic. Treated by Karin Lundgren and at the pain clinic.
Has a chronic headache without a known origin. Given Methadone, Actiqe and Stesolid.
Came to clinic on the 22/5 due to unsustainable situation with inadequate pain control.
Pat. is frustated over the long waiting time for the discontinuation of opiates which was to be done via IVA and planned by Dr. Torbjörn Andreasson.
Pat comes to NIVA and demands to be admitted to IVA and threatens to stop taking all drugs.
Pat had several conversations with PAL at Löwet, Sandra Månsson. Refers to previous notes.

Figure 1: An example of a pseudonymised electronic patient record written in Swedish (and its translation to English). It was judged as real by both evaluators. The text is relatively coherent, Mentioning places such as *Huddinge*, dates and date periods *20120311-20120318*, several personal names healthcare units such as *IVA*, Intensiv VårdsAvdelning (in Eng: Intensive Care Unit), *NIVA*, Neurologisk Intensiv VårdsAvdelning (in Eng: Neurological Intensive Care Unit) and *Löwet* a colloquial for Löwenströmska sjukhuset, (In Eng: Löwenströmska hospital) all of them pseudonymised. The underlinings have been added in this figure to show the PHI.

Entity	PHI-instance	Pseudo-nymised
First Name	923	-
Female First Name	-	364
Male First Name	-	555
Gender-neutral First Name	-	2
Last Name	929	929
Age	56	56
Phone Number	125	137
Location	148	148
Full Date	551	551
Date Part	711	711
Health Care Unit	1,025	1,026
Sum	**4,468**	**4,479**

Table 2: Types and numbers of all annotated PHI tokens in the Stockholm EPR PHI Corpus, replaced by the pseudonymisation program, the spell checker was used for nine males first names and ten females first names. (No social security number was found). The numbers are not matching completely. Location corresponds to all locations in Table 1.

Ny kontakt med smärtmottagning måndag. Närstående Mamma Madeleine tfn: 0652 7256 , Bror Madeleine tfn 078 1295067 Upplysning Får lämnas

In Eng:
New contact with pain clinic Monday. Related Mother Madeleine ph: 0652 7256 , Brother Madeleine ph 078 1295067 Inquiry May be given

Figure 2: An example of a pseudonymised electronic patient record written in Swedish that was correctly judged as pseudonymised by the senior evaluator by the agreement brother *Bror* and gender of the name of the brother *Madeleine* which is a female name. Also the mother *Mamma* has the same name *Madeleine* as the brother, which makes it confusing.

The two evaluators also judged incorrectly that two and one records respectively were pseudonymised, while they were non-pseudonymised records. In average only 3.5 percent of the psuedonymised records were correctly judged as psuedonymised and 1.5 percent of the non-pseudonymised records were wrongly judged as psuedonymised.

Concluding that 91 percent of the pseudonymised records were judged as original (or non-pseudonymised) records in average.

The senior evaluator obtained a precision of 67 percent and a recall of 10 percent. The junior evaluator obtained a precision of 75 percent and a recall of 8 percent. None of the pseudonymised records was judged as pseudonymised by both of the evaluators.

Some of the comments for reasons for revealing the records as pseudonymised were that the physician's name was strange, a brother with a female name, and also wrong gender, see Figure 2.

6 Discussion and conclusion

Many of the identified pseudonymised patient records were revealed because of strange combinations of first names and last names, for example, a Christian male first name and a Muslim last name such as *Peter Mohamed*, both separately common Swedish names. Another case was family relationships such as husband, wife, daughter or son combined with the wrong gender of the name. Another exemple was two dates that were too inconsistent in time, where the cause happens after the effect, also wrong type of healthcare unit mentioned for the specific disease the patient has. For example "bor permanent på Löwet", (In Eng: "Lives permanent at Löwet"), where *Löwet* is colloquial for "Löwenströmska sjukhuset", (In Eng: "Löwenströmska hospital"), and a patient does not usually live at a hospital but on a Geriatric unit or Residential home.

Also, the wrong preposition used for a location reveals that the records are pseudonymised, for example, prepositions in front of places and countries could pose problems since countries written in Swedish need the Swedish preposition *i* (English: in) while streets and islands require *på* (English: on).

The PHI tag *Location* is very general and covers everything from different locations (street, place, city, muncipality, country...), and in some cases organisations, companies or product names. The annotations for locations and healthcare units are basic and when pseudonymising them, strange combinations can occur. The generated phone numbers could in some case generate strange grouping of numbers.

The research question was whether a reader of an electronic patient record could reveal if one record was pseudonymised or not. The answer is no, hence a layperson reader probably cannot reveal to 91 percent that a record is pseudonymised or not. Probably a clinically trained person might reveal more, and adding external databases will ofcourse assist in revealing if the record is pseudonymised or not.

The results in this study are much more promising than the study by Björkegren (2016) where half of the randomly generated records that was pseudonymised were revealed as pseudonymised by the evaluators, in their case, three different evaluators evaluating the same 17 records were eight records were pseudonymised. One of the evaluator was a physician at Karolinska University Hospital, the two others were computer scientists.

The results are also in line with the results in (Meystre et al., 2014) where five physicians were asked if they could recognise their patient in 86 de-identified patient records and where none succeeded in this task.

The purpose of Hiding In Plain Sight (HIPS) to not reveal the un-annotated PHI can also be considered fulfilled.

Future research will be to improve the pseudonymisation program to diminish the number of bugs, but also to create common combinations of first and last names, checking the agreement for family relationship and the right gender of first names, for example, brother and the use of a male name and not a female name, etc. Solve the problem with the broad class *Location* by dividing it into the classes "real' locations and organisations.

The use of more general healthcare unit names and also improve the date shifting mechanisms, but also to make more significant variations of the produced vocabulary to make the pseudonymised data useful as training data for machine learning algorithms.

There is also research going on for generating synthetical patient records from real patient records, that does not contain any sensitive information. This method could be an entirely different way to go.

Acknowledgments

Great thanks to Panos Papapetrou and Isak Samsten for carrying out the evaluation of the electronic patient records texts. Thanks also to Andreas Amsenius that provided the special list for town squares and parks from earlier work on de-identifications of emails. and thanks also to André Antfolk and Rikard Branting that provided with list on locations that were organised hierarchically.

References

Alyaa Alfalahi, Sara Brissman, and Hercules Dalianis. 2012. Pseudonymisation of personal names and other PHIs in an annotated clinical Swedish corpus. In *Third Workshop on Building and Evaluating Resources for Biomedical Text Mining (BioTxtM 2012) held in conjunction with LREC 2012, May 26, Istanbul*, pages 49–54.

Andreé Antfolk and Rikard Branting. 2016. Pseudonymisering av platser i patientjournaltexter (In Swedish). Bachelor's thesis, Department of Computer and Systems Sciences, Stockholm University.

Andreas Björkegren. 2016. Pseudonymisering av digitala patientjournaler (In Swedish). Bachelor's thesis, Department of Computer and Systems Sciences, Stockholm University.

David Carrell, Bradley Malin, John Aberdeen, Samuel Bayer, Cheryl Clark, Ben Wellner, and Lynette Hirschman. 2013. Hiding in plain sight: use of realistic surrogates to reduce exposure of protected health information in clinical text. *Journal of the American Medical Informatics Association*, 20(2):342–348.

Hercules Dalianis. 2018. *Clinical Text Mining: Secondary Use of Electronic Patient Records*. Springer.

Hercules Dalianis and Sumithra Velupillai. 2010. De-identifying Swedish clinical text-refinement of a gold standard and experiments with Conditional random fields. *Journal of Biomedical Semantics*, 1:6.

Louise Deleger, Todd Lingren, Yizhao Ni, Megan Kaiser, Laura Stoutenborough, Keith Marsolo, Michal Kouril, Katalin Molnar, and Imre Solti. 2014. Preparing an annotated gold standard corpus to share with extramural investigators for de-identification research. *Journal of Biomedical Informatics*, 50:173–183.

Margaret Douglass, Gari D. Clifford, Andrew Reisner, George B. Moody, and Roger G. Mark. 2004. Computer-assisted de-identification of free text in the MIMIC II database. In *Computers in Cardiology, 2004*, pages 341–344. IEEE.

Cyril Grouin, Nicolas Griffon, and Aurélie Névéol. 2015. Is it possible to recover personal health information from an automatically de-identified corpus of french ehrs? In *Proceedings of the Sixth International Workshop on Health Text Mining and Information Analysis*, pages 31–39.

Stephane Meystre, Jeffrey Friedlin, Brett South, Shuying Shen, and Matthew Samore. 2010. Automatic de-identification of textual documents in the electronic health record: a review of recent research. *BMC Medical Research Methodology*, 10(1):70.

Stéphane M. Meystre, Shuying Shen, Deborah Hofmann, and Adi V. Gundlapalli. 2014. Can physicians recognize their own patients in de-identified notes? In *MIE-Medical Informatics Europe*, pages 778–782.

Latanya Sweeney. 1996. Replacing personally-identifying information in medical records, the scrub system. In *Proceedings of the AMIA annual fall symposium*, page 333. American Medical Informatics Association.

Özlem Uzuner, Yuan Luo, and Peter Szolovits. 2007. Evaluating the State-of-the-Art in Automatic De-identification. *Journal of the American Medical Informatics Association*, 14(5):550–563.

Sumithra Velupillai, Hercules Dalianis, Martin Hassel, and Gunnar H Nilsson. 2009. Developing a standard for de-identifying electronic patient records written in Swedish: precision, recall and F-measure in a manual and computerized annotation trial. *International Journal of Medical Informatics*, 78(12):e19–e26.

Association for Computational Linguistics
209 N. Eighth Street
Stroudsburg, Pennsylvania 18360

ISBN 978-1-5108-9445-7

9 781510 894457

CURRAN ASSOCIATES INC.
proceedings.com